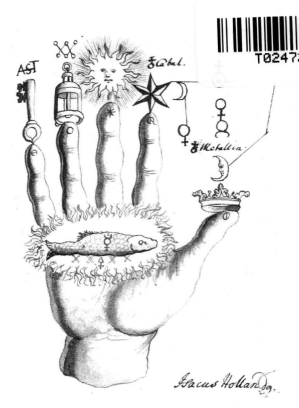

The Hand of the Philosophers. Secret signs and symbols from
the ancient art of Alchemy. 17th Century.

US edition © Wooden Books Ltd 2024
Published by Wooden Books LLC,
San Rafael, California

First published in the UK in 2018
by Wooden Books Ltd, Glastonbury, UK

Library of Congress Cataloging-in-Publication Data
Green, M.
Charms, Amulets, Talismans & Spells

Library of Congress Cataloging-in-Publication
Data has been applied for

ISBN-10: 1-952178-42-8
ISBN-13: 978-1-952178-42-9

Designed and typeset in Glastonbury, UK

Printed in India on FSC® certified papers by
Quarterfold Printabilities Pvt. Ltd.

CHARMS,
AMULETS, TALISMANS
& SPELLS

Marian Green

Of magic doors there is this:
You do not know them
even when you are going through them

Above: Unicorn with Mane. From "Historia Animalum" by Conrad Gesner, 1551. Unicorn horn, also known as alicorn, was an important part of Western medicine during the Middle Ages, with powerful antidotal and healing properties. By the Renaissance it was already one of the most expensive remedies and one of the most valuable royal assets. Unicorn horns (in fact often Narwhal tusks) could still be purchased at apothecaries as universal antidotes until the 18th century. Unicorn horn was used to create scepters and other royal objects, such as the "unicorn throne" of the Danish kings, the scepter and crown of the Austrian Empire, and the scabbard and the hilt of the sword of Charles the Bold.

CONTENTS

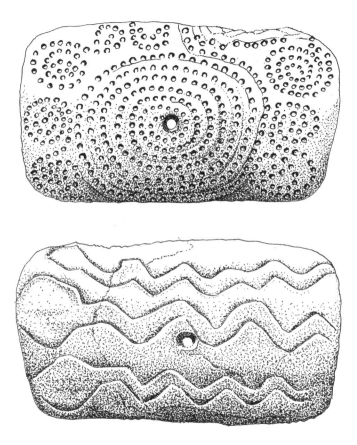

*Above: One of the earliest magical objects. Carved panel of mammoth
ivory, from Mal'ta, Siberia, c. 24,000 BC. Upper image: Seven spirals.
Lower image: Reverse side with three serpents.*

INTRODUCTION

PEOPLE HAVE ALWAYS collected or created objects with strange or beneficial properties. Archaeologists describe these ancient items as *charms* or *talismans* for magic or healing, and luck bringers or *amulets* to ward off harm. We still have "lucky charms" which we keep safe or attach to a variety of everyday objects. They are still used in natural and ritual magic and are found in all sorts of non-magical contexts.

Spells survive either in pure form or as spell-like chants, songs, and poems. Football teams have animal mascots and employ anthems from the crowd. Historic places sell souvenirs of Cornish piskies, holy water, or copies of magical objects.

Neanderthals decorated shells with ochre to wear as jewelery. Their cave art depicts breathtaking images of animals and birds, believed to be hunting magic, or to honor prey. Some people had gifts for finding food, fresh water, or shelter for their tribe long before villages were established. These survival skills are real magic—if the sorcerer's divinations failed, the tribe could starve. Today we don't need to rely on the wild for sustenance, but people still read their horoscopes, have lucky numbers or colors, horseshoes or prayers on a wall, cross their fingers for luck, or throw spilled salt over their shoulder to ward off harm. The old superstitions are an unconscious belief in magic.

All over the world, there are strange "cult objects," "spells" written in heiroglyphs, "phallic" carvings or "power" stones, requests to the Gods for justice or assistance, in places of worship, private homes, and museums. The ancient magical arts work!

THE ORIGINS OF MAGIC
and sacred objects

ANIMISM was a central feature of early human culture. Natural objects and entire landscapes (*see opposite*) had spirits or gods dwelling within. People interacted with these powers, by verbal supplication, threats, or offerings. At some point in the development of our species, there begins a shift toward worship and ritual. We moved away from direct communication with the unseen and sought mediation through specific deities and human-animal entities. Both approaches still exist.

The first charms were stones with holes through, fossils, or other strange-shaped natural objects (*opposite, below*). They kept, and keep us, linked to the original source of all that is magical.

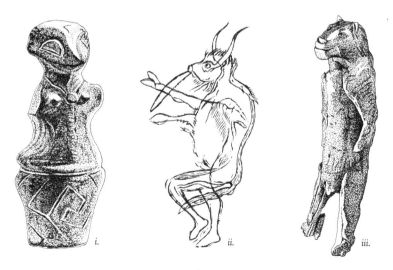

i.   ii.   iii.

ABOVE: *The landscape has always formed the basis for belief in and interaction with unseen spiritual forces. The shapes of rocks, a stream, trees, hills, or the horizon may suggest a dragon, bird, or reclining female figure, often considered a god, goddess, or elemental being of the place.*

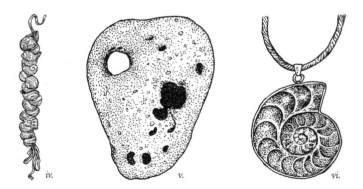

iv.   *v.*   *vi.*

FACING PAGE: *i. Goddess figure, Vinča culture, Transylvania, c. 5000 BC. ii. Bison-headed man, Le Gabillou Cave, France, 13,000 BC. iii. Lion-man, the earliest zoomorphic/anthropomorphic sculpture yet found, Stadel-Hohle cave, Swabian Alps, Germany, c. 30,000 BC. Above: iv. Snail shells, strung up like garlic to act as a fertility charm, 20th century. v. The holey, or holy, stone, could hold an ice crystal and act as a lens to make fire. vi: Spiral ammonites or "petrified snakes" are still worn as keepsakes or lucky charms today.*

ANCIENT MAGIC
foundations

The earliest surviving writing about magic is cuneiform. Sadly, for researchers, healing chants, protective spells, and words of power were never written down; instead early inscriptions tend to record the positions of stars and planets, mark boundaries, and proclaim rules.

Egyptian hieroglyphs tell us much more. Written on papyrus and carved on stone are gods, goddesses prayers, and protective spells. The oldest examples of written spells are found engraved on amuletic heart scarabs, symbols of rebirth and self-generation. The example shown (*below right*) asks the heart of the deceased person, upon whom it was placed, not to speak out when being judged in the afterlife.

When the Greeks overran Egypt they brought their own goddesses of wisdom and magic. The three-faced Hekate, like the Egyptian Heka, ruled the underworld and magical arts. She is often shown brandishing a torch. Dreams, sleep, death, and fate all had their own deities. People consulted oracular priestesses at Delphi where prophesies were made (*see p.48*). Aesclepius, god of healing (*opposite top right*), had temples where dreams were analyzed to find cures. His staff, entwined with a snake, is still used to show a pharmacy or clinic today.

LEFT: *Clay "map" of sheep's liver used in "extispicy" - reading the entrails, Babylon c. 2000 BC.* RIGHT: *Aesclepius, ancient Greek hero and God of Medicine, shown with staff and coiling snake, Romano-Bulgarian mosaic.*

ABOVE: *"The Cutting of the Mistletoe," showing druids surrounded by Roman soldiers on Anglesey. Opposite: Cuneiform tablet; top and bottom of a Scarab Beetle amulet with engraved heiroglyphic text.*

MEDIEVAL MAGIC
as above so below

The Medieval church rejected pagan beliefs—spells, divination, conjuring spirits, blood offerings, curses, and even healings were all suppressed or banned. Folk healers, village witches, and wizards were forced to practice their skills in secret. Alchemists who tried chemical experiments to make gold and useful drugs worked in hidden laboratories. However, *grimoires*, the textbooks of magical techniques, can still be found, and herbal knowledge, astrology, divination, and spell weaving are still widely practiced.

It was common to connect various herbs, flowers, edible, or useful plants and scents to the visible planets. People believed that the power of Venus would influence a charm made using rose petals, while eating strawberries and burning benzoin, bringing harmony and love. These connections between planetary powers, plants, and incenses are still used in casting spells, making charms, and designing talismans. Some common correspondences are shown opposite (*see too pages 13, 19 & 39*).

✦ PLANTS AND PLANETS ✦

		INCENSE	EDIBLE	FLOWER	HERB	TREE
☽	**MOON**	jasmine, willow, aloes	melon, cucumber, pumpkin, lettuce, mushrooms	white poppy, honeysuckle, valerian, lilies	nutmeg, bay, evening primrose	willow, eucalyptus, palm
♂	**MARS**	tobacco, camphor	carrot, spices, ginger, hot peppers, horseradish	corn, red poppy, hawthorn, madder	mustard, anise, basil, nettles, garlic, thistle, chives	holly, pine, blackthorn, hawthorn
☿	**MERCURY**	pine resin, sandalwood	celery, maize, fennel, garlic, parsnips, walnuts	dog's mercury, white bryony, verbena	mace, oregano, parsley, lavender, dill, fennel	acacia, almond, aspen, hazel
♃	**JUPITER**	cedar, violet, clove	chicory, figs, blackcurrant, asparagus	blue iris, blue lotus, dandelion	anise, melissa, borage, tansy, bay, chervil	chestnut, oak, fig, maple, horse chestnut
♀	**VENUS**	rose, benzoin, sage	apple, cherry, raspberries, strawberry	rose, daisy, meadowsweet, periwinkle	lovage, thyme, mint, mugwort, vanilla, yarrow	apple, birch, elder, lime, plum
♄	**SATURN**	myrrh, copal	black grape, blackberry, beetroot, olive	pansy, elderflowers, hellebore, cinquefoil, nightshade	rue, comfrey, fenugreek, mullein	beech, elm, alder, pine, yew, walnut
☉	**SUN**	frankincense, mastic gum	orange, ginger, melon, lemon, almond	sunflower, buttercup, daffodil, marigold	camomile, angelica, cinnamon, saffron	oak, almond, bay, olive, orange, cedar
⊕	**EARTH**	dittany of Crete	potatoes, carrot, beetroot, radish	all flowering plants	all medicinal & edible plants	all deciduous trees and shrubs

SUPERSTITIONS AND OMENS
fingers crossed

Omens are ominous signs of impending danger and warn of trouble ahead. Natural events like eclipses of sun or moon, or comets were once widely viewed with fear and trepidation. Superstitions can be widely held or be entirely personal, but most people do special things "for luck," such as wearing favored colors, avoiding certain actions like stepping on the lines of a pavement, or knocking on wood to cancel an unlucky action. Objects or images are often used as lucky mascots—Cornish piskeys, Irish shamrocks. Some of the more common superstitions and omens are listed (*opposite*).

Performers and athletes are notoriously superstitious and often exhibit a range of idiosyncratic rituals. Famous examples from the world of football include: being last onto the pitch, kissing/hitting the same teammate before every game, being the last player to put shorts on, and spitting on the pitch before taking a penalty.

ACORNS are symbols of immortality, as life springing forth from the earth.

AMBER is a form of fossilized tree resin, millions of years old, and beads are thought to prevent throat infections.

BATS are thought in the east to bring longevity, although in the west they are often viewed as being sinister.

BEES are used as charms to encourage prosperity as they gather sweet honey. They used to be told family news.

BIRDS can be seen as omens for trouble when a single magpie is seen, or for good luck in flights of odd numbers.

BLACK DOGS turn up in many folk tales as harbingers of doom, so no one should follow one at night.

BROOMS. Sweeping out the door after dusk was considered risky lest you sweep out all your luck.

CLOUDS are often interpreted as signs of wonder, their many shapes forming faces, angelic wings, and animals.

COMETS were traditionally thought to foretell great events, deaths of kings, or impending war.

CROWS and ravens were birds with positive interpretation, concerned with memory and forethought.

DOLPHINS were sacred to Apollo, a god of music and the arts, as well as forms of healing for mind and body.

DOVES are birds of Venus, the goddess of love. They were offered as sacrifices in Roman temples.

ECLIPSES made ancient peoples very uneasy as birds and animals behaved strangely in the sudden darkness.

EMBERS and burning logs were often used as a simple form of divination when images seen in the fireplace showed the future.

FINGERS CROSSED was a way of warding off harm, or wishing for a bit of good luck.

FROGS were looked upon as symbols of abundance due to the masses of frogspawn appearing from nowhere.

KNIVES and scissors were considered unlucky gifts as they could cut friendships, so it was customary for the recipient to give a small coin in exchange.

LADDERS. Walking under a ladder breaks the holy trinity and risks a bucket on the head.

MIRRORS often turn up in folk tales, like "Mirror, mirror on the wall, who is the fairest one of all?" where they could give a clear or murky reflection.

MACBETH, the Scottish play by Shakespeare, is viewed by many actors as extremely unlucky.

MAGPIES are birds whose number dictates good or ill fortune. "One for sorrow, two for joy ..." Seeing one alone suggests it has been widowed, as these birds mate for life.

RABBITS were regarded with extreme trepidation by fishermen, who, on seeing one, would return home, abandoning their voyage.

RAINBOWS signify a change for the better, being a sign to Noah that the flooding rains were ended.

RINGS were traditionally exchanged during a wedding, the unbroken circle indicating an unending union.

ROCKING CHAIRS set rocking when empty were considered an invitation to wandering spirits.

SALT, being an ancient preservative, is often used to purify a magical circle. To accidently spill salt, however, could presage bad luck, unless it was cast over the left shoulder to drive away harm.

SHEEP'S LIVER was in ancient times used for divination, with certain marks or blemishes indicating ill health.

SHOOTING STARS are considered to bring good luck, so when meteor showers are predicted people go into the night to watch and wonder.

WOOD, being a natural substance, has been used to connect with nature. It is still a superstition to touch or knock on wood to bring good luck.

How Magic Works
as within so without

Magical arts require a focused mind, a specific objective, and the patience to bring about your will. By changing your awareness of situations, through meditation and concentration, effective strategies may be formulated.

Charms, spells, and talismans, through many centuries of use, have proved to be effective tools to support this approach, but they work effectively only for *need*, not *greed*. They will often require the language and symbology of *correspondences* (*see below, & pages 7, 13, 19 & 39*) to awaken the attention of specific energies. Like a phone call, the line may be engaged, the deity unavailable, the signal weak, or you may have the wrong number. Patience is needed, for to move all the factors into the desired position may take time. You must be very certain what is required, select the symbols which best correspond to that need, and concentrate entirely on a successful outcome.

When it works properly, magic looks like coincidence.

CORRESPONDENCES OCCUR BETWEEN:

PLANET ~ ZODIACAL SIGN ~ DAY OF THE WEEK ~

MOON PHASE ~ SEASON ~ MONTH ~ HOUR ~

ALPHABET ~ LETTER ~ NUMBER ~ ANGEL ~ SPIRIT ~

ANIMAL ~ PLANT ~ METAL ~ MINERAL ~ STONE ~

HERB ~ FLOWER ~ PERFUME ~ COLOR ~ ELEMENT ~

ELEMENTAL ~ SHAPE ~ DEITY ~ TREE ~ RULER

11

Is Magic Dangerous?
elf and safety

Not all schemes go to plan. There are strict rules for magic to work successfully, often expressed in the phrase "If it harms none, do what you will." This is not easy. First you must discover your *true* will.

Magical ritual works on a mental, psychic, and material level. You use real water to purify, and a lit candle to consecrate, but your mind sees beyond the table set before you. It is this dislocation of awareness, trained through determined mental practice, that allows you to experience the presence of gods, angels or elemental powers—all of which are "real" in their own dimensions. If you don't complete your working honestly and with intent, these awakened images can seep into your dreams and waking hours to disrupt your life. They are not evil or harmful, but can be disturbing. Never use any technique you don't understand, or any that will change other people's lives. If acting on behalf of others, get their permission first.

There are a variety of different beings which can be called upon to be your partners in magical work, whether it be a spell, healing ritual, or a talisman being made for a specific purpose (*see table opposite*).

⇥ PLANETS, GODS, AND ANGELS ⇤

	MOON ☽	MARS ♂	MERCURY ☿	JUPITER ♃	VENUS ♀	SATURN ♄	SUN ☉
EGYPTIAN	Khons	Horus	Thoth	Amon	Bast	Isis	Ra
GREEK	Artemis	Ares	Hermes	Zeus	Aphrodite	Kronos	Apollon
ROMAN	Luna	Mars	Mercury	Jupiter	Venus	Saturn	Apollo
NORSE	Nanna	Thor	Bragi	Norns	Thor	Frigg	Frey
CELTIC	Epona	Morrigan	Lugh	Taranis	Morrigan	Ceridwen	Bel
ANGEL	Gabriel	Samael	Raphael	Sachiel	Hanael	Cassiel	Michael
MAGIC	Dream	Action	Communication	Job/Law	Love/Friendship	Patience	Health/Self
VIRTUE	Independence	Courage	Honesty	Obedience	Generosity	Silence	Devotion
VICE	Idleness	Cruelty	Dishonesty	Hypocracy	Lust	Avarice	Pride
SPHERE	Foundation	Strength	Glory	Mercy	Victory	Understanding	Beauty

ABOVE: Table showing major European (and Egyptian) deities, as well as angels and the realms of magic where they can be most helpful. The planets and their powers, virtues, and spheres of action can be invited to empower talismans, visualized in meditation, or seen in dreams to confirm your spell or talisman is working. Always be polite and patient when asking assistance from Gods and Angels. Be aware they are your allies.

LEFT: Summoning. Spirits and angels are individual living beings who can be invited to assist with any spell, make a charm effective or an amulet protective by choosing the appropriate day of the week and magical hour, wearing the corresponding color, and burning the right incense. They may also refuse to help. They cannot be bribed or coerced into obeying you.

PLANT MAGIC
meals, mushrooms, and medicine

Plants have always been important in magic. They can be eaten as ordinary food, or can be employed for their occult or healing properties. Most plants, from tiny herbs to trees (*see opposite*), have time-tested connections to gods and supernatural beings. Many people also connect directly with these entities or heal with *plant spirit medicine* (often passed down from ancient tribal traditions).

Charms can be made from twigs and fruits woven into sacred patterns. Dowsing rods were traditionally cut from willow or hazel to help diviners find water. Wizards carried magical staffs, while sorcerers had wands and witches had besoms. All these instruments control power and were always made by the user from trees which were sacred to them. Roots, flowers, bark, leaves, fungi, and stems may be used in potions, each connecting to a particular planet (*see p.7*). You could carry some dried mint in your wallet to ensure a mint of money, or some sage for wisdom.

There is also a secret code of flowers and plants which can be used to send messages to recipients who understand the symbolism.

A Turnip.

A Radish.

A Parsnip.

⇸ MAGICAL TREE LORE ⇷

	SPIRIT	MATTER
ASH	In Norse mythology Yggdrasil is commonly believed to be an immense ash tree, sacred to Odin and source of all runes.	Leaves can be used as a tonic for horses, its wood is good for tool handles, staffs, and royal thrones. An exceptional wood to burn.
ELDER	A tree with strong feminine associations and embodying the "Elder-mother." In many traditions it was forbidden to cut down elder.	Cooling and soothing leaves. Wear them inside shoes if walking long distances. Both flowers and berries make excellent wine.
OAK	The most holy of trees in Britain and Ireland. Its acorns symbolize fertility. Pliny noted that Druids performed all sacred rites in oak groves.	Feeds many valuable insects, protects against lightning, bark used in tanning leather. Many early Christian churches built of oak.
YEW	Signifies everlasting life, death, and rebirth (branches grow down into ground and form new "trunks").	The longest growing European tree. The seeds are poisonous but the fruit around them is edible. Used to make longbows.
HOLLY	Tree of hope during the dark days of winter. Often seen as a "King" with ivy as the "Queen." Romans held it sacred to Saturn.	Features in scores of ancient rituals and festivities including Christmas, Easter, and St. Stephen's day. Burn holly to signify death of winter.
HAWTHORN	Once known simply as "May," it has strong associations with Beltane. First leaves heal the heart. "N'ere cast a clout 'til May be out!"	Ancient Greek girls wore hawthorn crowns at weddings. Many traditions ban the flowers from entering the house.
HAZEL	Linked to knowledge, wisdom, and the pagan "Otherworld." For the Romans it was sacred to Mercury. Often found by holy wells.	Used to make dowsing rods, poles for benders, hurdles, walking sticks, besom handles, forked staffs, and much more.
WILLOW	Revered in many traditions. Orpheus touched a willow sacred to Persephone. Ishtar's predecessor, Belili, was know as the "willow mother."	The bark is used to tie up spells and can also be made into magical whistles. Aspirin can be made from its bark.
ROWAN	A protective tree. Especially sacred in Scotland. Scottish fairies said to gather within stone circles protected by rowan.	Tradition confers strict rules around its use. Spinning wheels and spindles made from rowan in Scotland and Ireland.
APPLE	The apple (or silver) branch was a key to faeryland, and a passport for safe return. Mythic Avalon was also known as "The Isle of Apples."	Fruit for sustenance and medicine. Unsweetened apple juice is an effective digestive cleanser. Apple cider vinegar has myriad healing properties.
BIRCH	Protective and symbolic of new beginnings. Strips of bark were used to write spells on.	Twigs were used to make besom bristles. Maypoles were often birch wood.
BEECH	The tree of writing. The words "book" and "bible" both come from beech.	Beech nuts (mast) are loved by squirrels and, in kinder times, were used to fatten pigs.

Animal Magic
friends, fiends, and familiars

It has long been acknowledged that animals have augmented perceptions. Dogs can sense when their owners are coming home, birds react before earthquakes. As with their human counterparts, many also have a magical life, and have long been asscociated with planetary and other forces (*see opposite*). Many creation myths describe members of our species raised by animals—Romulus and Remus were famously suckled by a she-wolf.

Pets were uncommon in the middle ages. Dogs were for herding and guarding, and ladies living in cold castles kept lap dogs as living hot water bottles. Bats were feared for their nocturnal flight and hedgehogs were supposed to drink milk from cows lying down in fields. Cats kept as pets were thought to be familiar spirits that witches could send out to gather information or cause harm. This, however, is a mere footnote in the feline mythos—along with the serpent, cats have an incredible range of magical and symbolic associations stretching back millennia. A few are shown opposite. (*See too table on page 39.*)

LEFT: *The cat as Egyptian deity Bast, a Goddess/mother figure protecting her young.* CENTER: *The cosmic kitty, Ra (depicted as a cat), slaying the serpent Apep.* RIGHT: *A cat with the dead. Gallo-Roman tomb.*

LEFT: *Norse Goddess Freya, who ruled over 9 worlds, with a chariot drawn by 9-life cats.* CENTER: *Modern Hispanic & Chinese cat amulets.* RIGHT: *In oriental folklore, images of cats are hung to promote rest.*

Far left: Cat-eared jester holding the moon. Cats have long been connected with the moon, the night, femininity, and virginity.

Left: The Jaguar car logo magically associates the sleek power of the wild animal with the manufactured item.

FACING PAGE: *An animal alphabet. In the United Kingdom black cats are thought to be lucky if one crosses your path, whereas in the United States of America it is white cats that are considered fortunate.*

CHARMS
stones and bones

Charms are objects, found or adapted, which bring good fortune. They can take many forms. They may have been blessed or infused with power by coming from a specific location, like a pebble from a healing spring or a sprig of a sacred tree. Or they may be infused with deeper meaning through tradition and folklore (a holey stone used to be hung above a horse's stable to ward off unwanted influences). Charms may be carried around or placed somewhere meaningful.

Many people still pick up interestingly shaped stones or crystals. Rose quartz is found on Cornish beaches, jet in East Anglia, and garnets in the Scottish highlands. Importantly, every gem also has links to birth signs and planetary powers (*see table opposite*).

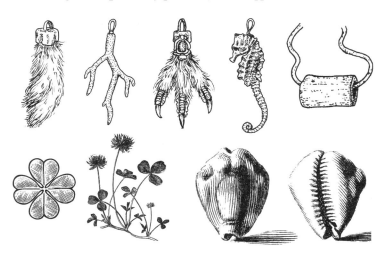

✦ STONES & CRYSTALS ✦

Sign	Planet	Element	Stone or Crystal	Magical Notes
ARIES	Mars	Fire (cardinal)	Ancient: Bloodstone, Amethyst. Modern: Diamond, Aventurine, Aquamarine.	AGATE heals, tones & lends courage. AMETHYST focuses the mind. AMETRINE cleans & energises.
TAURUS	Venus	Earth (fixed)	Ancient: Emerald. Modern: Carnelian, Malachite, Rose Quartz.	AQUAMARINE clarifies and lends hope. AVENTURINE clears fear and anxiety. BLOODSTONE purifies and clears.
GEMINI	Mercury	Air (mutable)	Ancient: Agate. Modern: Apophyllite, Celestite, Chrysocolla, Serpentine.	CALCITE calms and reduces stress. CARNELIAN protects against wounds. CITRINE brings hope and well-being.
CANCER	Moon	Water (cardinal)	Ancient: Ruby. Modern: Calcite, Moonstone, Natrolite, Rhodizite.	CRYSOCOLLA for joy and communication. DIAMOND purifies and protects. EMERALD aids dreams & visions.
LEO	Sun	Fire (fixed)	Ancient: Onyx. Modern: Amber, Citrine, Kunzite, Sunstone, Petalite, Golden Topaz.	FLUORITE removes confusion. GARNET enhances the imagination. HEMATITE soothes frayed nerves.
VIRGO	Mercury	Earth (mutable)	Ancient: Garnet. Modern: Amazonite, Crysocolla, Moss Agate, Stichite, Zircon.	JADE connects to divine love. JET aids scrying and divination. KUNZITE brings happiness & self esteem.
LIBRA	Venus	Air (cardinal)	Ancient: Sapphire. Modern: Ametrine, Chrysoprase, Lepidolite, Tanzanite.	LAPIS LAZULI opens psychic skills. LEPIDOLITE for light, joy and sleep. MALACHITE brings health & prosperity.
SCORPIO	Pluto (Mars)	Water (fixed)	Ancient: Peridot. Modern: Boji Stone, Charoite, Kunzite, Labradorite, Turquoise.	MAGNETITE extends your psyche. OBSIDIAN grounds & dispels negativity. ONYX brings self control.
SAGITTARIUS	Jupiter	Fire (mutable)	Ancient: Lapis Lazuli. Modern: Azurite, Dioptase, Obsidian, Herkimer, Tanzanite.	OPAL brings magic and visions. PERIDOT for intuition & good luck. QUARTZ clears and amplifies.
CAPRICORN	Saturn	Earth (cardinal)	Ancient: Garnet. Modern: Tourmaline, Aragonite, Fluorite, Jet, Magnetite.	ROSE QUARTZ will heal most ills. RUBY is for power and movement. SAPPHIRE enhances psychic love.
AQUARIUS	Uranus (Saturn)	Air (fixed)	Ancient: Amethyst. Modern: Angelite, Cryolite, Garnet, Hematite, Merlinite.	SERPENTINE connects to nature. TOPAZ soothes and brings peace. TOURMALINE grounds and balances.
PISCES	Neptune (Jupiter)	Water (mutable)	Ancient: Aquamarine. Modern: Ametrine, Bluelace Agate, Fluorite, Opal, Turquoise.	TURQUOISE for creativity & friendship. ZIRCON heals and aids sleep.

FACING PAGE, FROM TOP LEFT: A rabbit's foot (left hind) is lucky in west Africa; Coral is worn for luck in Mediterranean countries; Chicken's feet are used in Voodoo, Hoodoo, and Juju for protection against theft; Seahorse charm to ward off evil; Holey stones are powerful protectors; Four-leafed clovers symbolize the holy trinity (faith, hope, and charity) plus one for luck; Sea shells purify water for simple rituals.

MAKING CHARMS
and counting your luck

If you can't find an object which you believe to be lucky, you can instead make one or buy one. Overt or stylized representations of animals or objects, both natural and man-made, can easily become analogues for the real thing (*see opposite*).

People still wear charm bracelets adorned with silver or gold tokens, lucky horsehoes, crosses, mementoes of places visited, and symbols of personal affection. For many, tattoos serve the same function. Like superstitions (*see pages 8-9*) any object or symbol can become a personal charm through use and perceived efficacy. Good luck and love charms may be given as gifts, and strange objects loaded with arcane symbolism may be bequeathed to family members—gold coins and bank notes are often especially welcomed.

Numbers have magical power too. They can be lucky, unlucky, or sacred. To find your personal *Name Lucky Number*, write it out with the values given below for each letter, then add these up until you get a single digit. As shown in the example (*below right*), you can also add up the date, month, and year of your birth in the same way to arrive at your *Birth Lucky Number*.

1	2	3	4	5	6	7	8	9
A	B	C	D	E	F	G	H	I
J	K	L	M	N	O	P	Q	R
S	T	U	V	W	X	Y	Z	

$$M\ I\ C\ H\ A\ E\ L \quad A\ N\ G\ E\ L\ O\ N$$
$$4\ 9\ 3\ 8\ 1\ 5\ 3 \quad 1\ 5\ 7\ 5\ 3\ 6\ 5$$
$$= (4+9+3+8+1+5+3) + (1+5+7+5+3+5+6)$$
$$= 33 + 32 = 3+3+3+2$$
$$= 11 = 1+1 = \mathbf{2}$$
$$05.07.1985 = 35 = 3+5 = \mathbf{8}$$

ABOVE: A silver charm bracelet with symbols, lucky charms, and mementoes gathered over many years.
BELOW: Cherubs adorn garlands with flowers, fruit, and leaves, similar to Christmas decorations today.

SPOKEN CHARMS
charming and whispering

Being charming works wonders—body language, movement, and gentle vocalization can calm or stir people and animals. Horse whisperers adopt body postures shown by other horses to befriend or challenge unbroken animals, while grooms often sing or whistle with working horses to encourage and reassure them (*and see cobras opposite*).

A *charm to cure warts* is said by a wartcharmer over the warty person: *Wart, wart, black of heart, I command you to depart!* Other forms of wart charming involve rubbing something on to each wart, and burying it to let it rot and cause the warts to disappear too. Bits of meat, or a live snail, pieces of string with a knot for each wart, or even coins may be touched to each blemish and then cast away. In *Macbeth* Shakespeare's witches teach us another trick: *Peace, the Charm's wound up.* This means that once the charm is said, time may be needed for the magic to work.

Rudyard Kipling's *A Charm* describes how to charm the dead: *Of English earth take thou as much as either hand may rightly clutch, and as you take it breathe a prayer for all who lie beneath.*

Charming things are attractive, alluring, enchanting, and enticing.

ABOVE: Snake-charmers in India sway and play their instruments to hypnotize the cobras.
BELOW: Witches practice speaking their magical spells, in this watercolor by Arthur Rackham.
OPPOSITE PAGE: Guido Fawkes and others in the Gunpowder Plot whispering their dangerous ideas.

THE POWER OF SYMBOLS
everything is one

Symbols of the sun or moon, of the ancient clockwise swastika or hexagram, of angels and animals carved into stonework or worn as pendants (*see opposite*) all act as passive protectors for the people and places they adorn. They are still used today in amuletic jewelry, trinkets, keyrings, and heraldry—anywhere where defensive qualities and other desired attributes need to be conveyed with visual succinctness.

Powerful images are often constructed from a number of symbolic elements combined into one potent talisman. Writing itself has also long been considered magical, with spells sometimes written in forgotten or antique scripts or languages to add power.

FACING PAGE: *Symbols used by Alchemists to represent the various minerals and metals used in their craft.*
ABOVE: *Images used in Heraldry on Coats of Arms, and worldwide religious and mystical symbols.*

25

AMULETS
patterns of protection

Varied in form and substance, amulets are objects or devices used principally for protection against harm, misfortune, or the "evil eye." Unlike talismans, which are made for a specific purpose, amulets can be bought and carried or displayed for continuous general protection.

Amulets are often flat disks, of metal, wood, or bone, with diagrams or symbols on them. They are worn or carried about one's person to provide passive but ceaseless defense. Some of the most enduring are based on ancient hand and eye motifs. The Hand of Fatima or *Hamsa/ Khamsa (opposite top center)* and the ancient Egyptian Eye of Horus *(opposite)* are still widely displayed in the Middle East and North Africa.

Others are carefully prepared sigils (personalized emblems with specific meaning/intent, *see pages 36-37*) or images carved by a magician to control unseen entities or protect from evil during the working of deep magic. Medals depicting Catholic saints are amulets, as are sacred Hebrew or Arabic texts inscribed on precious metal, worn or fixed to doorposts. The *Key of Solomon* (a magical grimoire attributed to King Solomon) contains many diagrams containing ancient symbols and languages; these can used to make powerful amulets (also refered to as *pentacles* or *seals*). An example is shown *(below right)*.

ABOVE LEFT: *Norse or Icelandic rune amulet.*   Center: *The Hand of Fatima, a popular Islamic symbol of protection.*   Above right: *Modern manufactured amulet with Qabalistic symbols.*

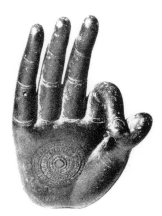

LEFT, UPPER: *Hand of Buddha mudra.* ABOVE: *Hebrew terracotta "Devil Trap" amulet with an engraved spell against the evil eye.* LEFT, LOWER: *The Eye of Horus, a powerful, multi-layered symbol from ancient Egypt, often used as a protective symbol.* FACING PAGE: LEFT: *A seven-pointed star amulet; an Eastern Bagua charm with Yin/Yang and trigrams; an amulet with planetary sigils.*

ANCIENT AMULETS
and their magical power

Often amulets which are designed to be carried about are drawn on parchment with symbols and writing which may not be easily understood. Some are engraved on metal to be worn as a necklace, or on finger rings, either outside, to be visible, or on the inside in secret. All kinds of symbols, sigils, and saints have amuletic powers within different traditions and cultures (*see opposite*).

Amulets can also be parts of buildings or boats. Knockers on doors in shapes of hands, faces, or imps ward off danger or make the mal-intentioned think twice. Gargoyles not only shoot out rain water, but are supposed to keep harmful energies away (*hunkypunks* only do the latter). Many of the carvings found on churches or old buildings are designed to be defensive. The S-shape of iron strengthening bars is a Norse rune used to ward off lightning.

Although most ancient amulets use symbols (*see illustrations opposite*), the very letters of many alphabets have been used for protection. In its most simple form this could be a red triangular notice: "Danger! Keep out!"; or "Beware of Falling Rocks." We are today surrounded by warnings and safety notices, the modern form of amulets.

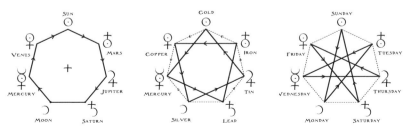

MEDIÆVAL TALISMANS.   EGYPTIAN TALISMANS.   EGYPTIAN TALISMANS.

ABOVE: *Ancient metal objects with defensive powers, including medieval and Egyptian ones which can be carried or worn as rings.*   BELOW: *Silver charms showing protective gods and sacred animals, stars, and fertility symbols. Opposite page: Signs of the planets and their metals & days, used in amulets and talismans.*

INDIAN AND THIBETAN TALISMANS.   PRIMEVAL, CHINESE, INDIAN AND THIBETAN TALISMANS.   ETRUSCAN, GREEK, ROMAN, AND ORIENTAL TALISMANS.

FERTILITY AND FECUNDITY
sex, drugs, and rock & roll

The need for fertility, whether in humans, animals, or crops, has always been an area where magical or religious assistance has been sought, often by carving, molding, or finding objects in the form of the phallus or vagina. Some of these are natural pebbles of a pillar shape, or stones with holes through, or knots in wood.

Museums hold a great number of fertility amulets, both as phallic symbols (particularly important to the Romans who used them as lamps and as pendants) and female goddess images (*see opposite*). Examples from the Mediterranean area vary between tiny carved women to the vast pregnant female figures of stone age Malta with their fat bellies and enlarged breasts. These fertility goddesses are some of the earliest representations of human beings.

The birth-giving figure of a *sheila-na-gig* is found over some church doors, while in other places the vesica pisces shape is used more subtly. Another mysterious figure thought to symbolize fecundity is the Green Man, or sometimes woman, whose face adorns many churches and secular buildings. The leaves sprouting from the face indicate the return of spring after winter, of fruits to come. Many of these foliate faces are wreathed with medicinal herbs and magical or edible plants.

MAKES GARMENTS AUSPICIOUS

BRINGS SUCCESS, WEALTH, LONG LIFE

SECURES THE HELP OF GOOD SPIRITS

MAKES BUSINESS SUCCESSFUL

MAKES TRAVELING SAFE

TOP LEFT: *Archaic goddess amulets, often set in shrines.* ABOVE: *Roman phallic amulet.* LEFT: *Goddess from Malta, 3000 BC.* BELOW LEFT: *Shela-na-gig from Kilpeck church, Herefordshire.* BELOW CENTER: *Green man door knocker, brings good luck with every visitor.* BELOW RIGHT: *Artichoke carving, used to bless a gateway.* FACING PAGE: *Miscellaneous amulets.*

TALISMANS
the making of wishes

In contrast to amulets, which are always "on," talismans are generally made with expert knowledge for a specific need. They are the most complicated and varied of magical items, often consecrated to be most effective at certain times, on particular days or during exact astrological or lunar periods (*see following page*). They can also be designed to work at a distance, either in time or in space. The word "talisman" indicates a magical object that works at a distance ("tele" = at a distance, "man" = manufactured). It can get confusing if a talisman is made with amuletic or protective features, such as John Dee's wax seal (*opposite top left*), but in general the above differences hold true.

Often used in ritual magic (the origin of the word in Greek links to *ceremony*), talismans are highly symbolic and embody requests for help from heavenly, geomantic, or intermediatory forces. The examples below show the magic squares of the seven planets. Steps within these squares then describe other occult symbols (*shown on page 39*).

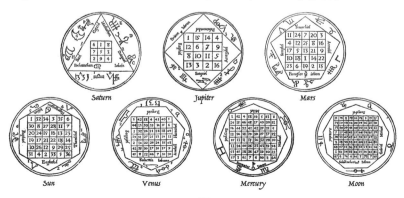

Saturn   Jupiter   Mars

Sun   Venus   Mercury   Moon

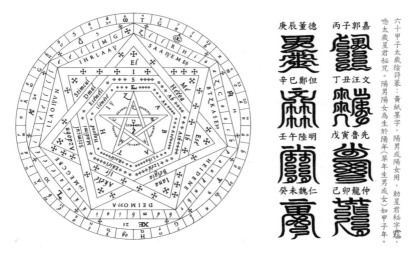

LEFT: *Wax talisman used by Dr. John Dee to protect his scrying rituals.* RIGHT: *Taisui talismans are popular at Chinese New Year for appeasing Tai Sui, the Grand Duke Jupiter, or New Year God.*

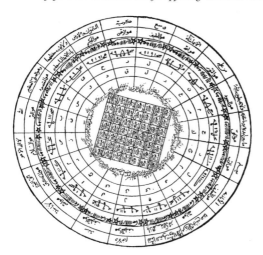

LEFT: *A da'ira talisman drawn by the Báb, founder of the Iranian Bábí faith. According to the Báb, this elaborate Iranian talisman for women calls upon planetary powers, angelic forces, and the hidden influences of written characters to bring about a positive outcome to the talisman maker's objective. Set within a solar circle divided into 19 and using a 7 by 7 number square, as well as magical letters, astrological positions, and numbers, this example demonstrates just how complicated making a talisman can be.*

DESIGNING A TALISMAN
what, when, and where

To make a talisman, first *think very deeply* about its exact purpose. Magical work tends to be literal, you get what you ask for. Thus money, as a means to a purpose, is not an apt subject. Decide if you wish to make a long or short term talisman. Then choose the planet(s) which best represent your purpose, and metals, colors, angelic names, incenses, sigils, numbers, and deities (*see tables on p.7, 13, 15, 19, 20, 39*) to symbolize protection, love, strength, healing, travel, and psychic ability.

Bring together the correct materials at the appropriate hour of the appropriate day (*see p.28 & table of hours below*), in a symbolic setting. This trains the magician's mind and makes the talisman a success.

	UNEVEN HOURS	E.G. AT EQUINOX	SUNDAY	MON	TUES	WED	THUR	FRI	SAT
	1st	6.00 AM	Sun	Moon	Mars	Mercury	Jupiter	Venus	Saturn
	2nd	7.00 AM	Venus	Saturn	Sun	Moon	Mars	Mercury	Jupiter
HOURS	3rd	8.00 AM	Mercury	Jupiter	Venus	Saturn	Sun	Moon	Mars
OF	4th	9.00 AM	Moon	Mars	Mercury	Jupiter	Venus	Saturn	Sun
THE	5th	10.00 AM	Saturn	Sun	Moon	Mars	Mercury	Jupiter	Venus
DAY	6th	11.00 AM	Jupiter	Venus	Saturn	Sun	Moon	Mars	Mercury
	7th	12.00 AM	Mars	Mercury	Jupiter	Venus	Saturn	Sun	Moon
(dawn	8th	1.00 PM	Sun	Moon	Mars	Mercury	Jupiter	Venus	Saturn
to	9th	2.00 PM	Venus	Saturn	Sun	Moon	Mars	Mercury	Jupiter
sunset)	10th	3.00 PM	Mercury	Jupiter	Venus	Saturn	Sun	Moon	Mars
	11th	4.00 PM	Moon	Mars	Mercury	Jupiter	Venus	Saturn	Sun
	12th	5.00 PM	Saturn	Sun	Moon	Mars	Mercury	Jupiter	Venus
	1st	6.00 PM	Jupiter	Venus	Saturn	Sun	Moon	Mars	Mercury
	2nd	7.00 PM	Mars	Mercury	Jupiter	Venus	Saturn	Sun	Moon
HOURS	3rd	8.00 PM	Sun	Moon	Mars	Mercury	Jupiter	Venus	Saturn
OF	4th	9.00 PM	Venus	Saturn	Sun	Moon	Mars	Mercury	Jupiter
THE	5th	10.00 PM	Mercury	Jupiter	Venus	Saturn	Sun	Moon	Mars
NIGHT	6th	11.00 PM	Moon	Mars	Mercury	Jupiter	Venus	Saturn	Sun
	7th	12.00 PM	Saturn	Sun	Moon	Mars	Mercury	Jupiter	Venus
(sunset	8th	1.00 AM	Jupiter	Venus	Saturn	Sun	Moon	Mars	Mercury
to	9th	2.00 AM	Mars	Mercury	Jupiter	Venus	Saturn	Sun	Moon
dawn)	10th	3.00 AM	Sun	Moon	Mars	Mercury	Jupiter	Venus	Saturn
	11th	4.00 AM	Venus	Saturn	Sun	Moon	Mars	Mercury	Jupiter
	12th	5.00 AM	Mercury	Jupiter	Venus	Saturn	Sun	Moon	Mars

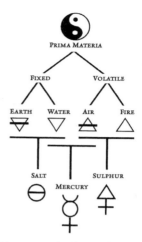

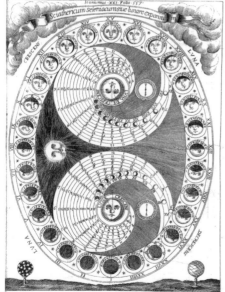

TOP LEFT: *Medieval images showing the interaction of the Sun and the Earth through the year, indicated by the Signs of the Zodiac.*

ABOVE: *The most common factors called upon when making talismans are the elements of Earth, Water, Fire, and Air (with Spirit often considered the fifth element). The ancient Greeks held that all matter was made up of these elements in varying proportions, and they also combined to create salt, sulphur, and mercury. Today physicists view everything as made from particles, waves, and energy.*

LEFT: *17th–century depiction of the phases of the Moon through a lunar month in relation to the Sun and Earth. The Moon's phase and season are important in making talismans.*

TALISMAN ESSENTIALS
planet, shape, color, metal

We can now consider the unseen and symbolic elements that you will use to make the talisman. The powers of the planets—traditionally the Sun, the Moon, Venus, Mercury, Mars, Jupiter, and Saturn—provide a good starting point. The earliest written records are of movements of these visible lights in the night sky, naming them as gods and goddesses, in all ancient civilizations. Each planet has acquired a collection of attributes like metals, colors, angels, incenses, numbers, and deities (*see opposite and pages 7 and 13*). They symbolize concepts like energy, love, courage, healing, travel, and psychic ability. Establish the link between your purpose and the planetary or other powers that will be called upon. Often one planet may be combined with the color, number, or shape of another to add an extra dimension of focus to any paper talisman. A blue Jupiter talisman might be written in solar gold ink and enclosed in a golden envelope. Mars" energy and force might be balanced by cooperating Venus, using red and green together.

Talismans attract beneficial energies by using the language of traditional symbols, powers, and objectives.

Magick Seals or Talismans.

The Seal of Saturn — Lead / Seal of Jupiter — Tin / Seal of Mars — Iron / Seal of the Sun — Gold / Seal of Venus — Copper / Seal of Mercury — Silver

⇀ MAGICAL SHAPES, SIGILS, AND COLORS ↽

PLANET	SHAPE	SEAL OF CHARACTER	SIGIL OF INTELLIGENCE	SIGIL OF SPIRIT	METAL / COLOR	ANIMAL	DAY / NUM. / PERFUME
MOON					Silver White Pearl Moonstone	Dog Cat Duck Chameleon	Monday 2 Aloes Frankincense
MERCURY					Mercury Orange Magenta Citrine	Fox Weasel Hare Lark	Wednesday 3 Mastic Cloves
VENUS					Copper Green Turquoise Emerald	Goat Dove Dolphin Grasshopper	Friday 5 Musk Rose
SUN					Gold Yellow Topaz Sunstone	Lion Bull Eagle Beetle	Sunday 1 Sandal Myrrh
MARS					Iron Red Ruby Garnet	Wolf Wild Pig Hawk Wasp	Tuesday 4 Pepper Cypress
JUPITER					Tin Brass Purple Blue Sapphire	Deer Elephant Pelican Eagle	Thursday 6 Nutmeg Saffron
SATURN					Lead Black Tourmaline Amethyst	Bear Scorpion Snake Tortoise	Saturday 8 Sulphur Turpentine

CREATING A TALISMAN
concentrate and consecrate

Before you begin the actual making, spend time in meditation within a sacred space. Indoors or out, in an old building or your own home, it is advisable to physically clear a place to work, not only to provide a table to work on, but also to make space inside yourself so you can focus on your task, quietly and undisturbed by anything or anyone.

Usually a sacred area is protected by symbols of the elements of Earth/north, Water/west, fire/south, and Air/east, which can be a stone, a bowl of spring water, a lighted candle or an electric one and some scented flowers or a joss stick for air (*see the blessing invocations opposite*). You will also need a colored card and pens.

Place the elemental symbols and then walk in a circle within them clockwise three times, mentally brushing away anything that will disturb you. Sit for a few moments reviewing what you intend to do and achieve. You will feel a calmness surrounding you.

Take the card for the talisman and cut it to the correct shape, then after a few moments, write clearly and concisely what you are asking for. Be sure you have thought this through. Place the new talisman on a clean cloth, ideally silk, and take it to each element in turn, asking a blessing. Place the talisman in the center again and ask the planet, god, or power to make it work. Sit in silence again, then wrap and hide your talisman for safekeeping. It should feel different. Thank each of the elements and snuff out the candle, and put everything away. This circle blessing can be used before any magical work.

Talismans should be destroyed once they have worked.

USES OF TALISMANS

Some talismans are for immediate or short term use, designed to achieve a specific goal:

* To get a new job (Jupiter)
* To sell or buy a new house (Sun)
* To solve an immediate problem (see list of planets and their specialities)
* To have a safe journey (Mercury)
* To set or maintain boundaries (Saturn)
* To have courage to sort out a problem, go to the dentist, or face an awkward neighbour (Mars)

Some Talismans are designed for long term or enduring use:

* To protect your children (Venus)
* To ask blessing on yourself (the Sun)
* To recall your dreams/Sleep well (the Moon)
* Achieve success at an ongoing project (Mercury)
* To be protected from harm or illness (Usually a God/Goddess or angelic power)

TALISMAN FOR DEFENSE
MARS WILL HELP YOU FEEL SAFE

1. Make your magic circle on a Tuesday (see page 28), during a waxing moon.
2. Write "I wish to feel safe in my daily life" on red card shaped like a pentagon, and include an image of your defensive animal, e.g. dragon.
3. Wrap it in silver foil.
4. Make a prayer to Mars (or the angel St. Michael, see page 13) to grant your desire.
5. Drink a sip of red wine (or anything red, see page 39) and pour some as a libation.
6. Imagine the talisman making a ring of steel as you carry it with you.
7. Close your circle.

LUNAR SLEEP TALISMAN
TO CURE INSOMNIA

1. Make your magic circle on a Monday (see p.28), after sunset, during a waning moon.
2. Write "I wish to sleep more peacefully" on white card shaped like a crescent moon (use silver ink if you can, see page 39).
3. Wrap it in silver foil.
4. Make a prayer to Hypnos to grant your desire.
5. Drink a sip of milk (or wine/honey water) and pour some as a libation.
6. Arrange some white flowers and meditate on peaceful sleep.
7. Close your circle.

SIGILS AND BIND RUNES
special seals and symbols

In many ancient grimmoires, the grammars of magic, strange Sigils appear, derived from one of the magical number squares (*Kameas, shown on pages 32 & 38*), used to call attention of a particular planetary spirit. Through spelling out the spirit's name by connecting the letters a sigil is formed. Often modern spell weavers create a personal sigil, rather like the "tags" used by graffiti painters to sign their work.

To make a personal sigil you can take your whole name, magical name, or initials in the Latin alphabet and place the letters on top of each other. This will form the basis of a sigil, but you need to simplify it to make a pleasing pattern. This can be used as your personal magical seal, to sign spells, mark books, and identify magical tools.

The Norse runes (*opposite top*) are used as letters for spells, as individual protective charms, and as magical symbols for divination (*other magical alphabets for spells are shown on page 44*).

א	ב	ג	ד	ה	ו	ז	ח	ט
ALEPH (A) 1	BETH (B) 2	GIMEL (G) 3	DALETH (D) 4	HE (H) 5	VAU (V) 6	ZAYIN (Z) 7	CHETH (CH) 8	TETH (T) 9
י	כּ	ל	מ	נ	ס	ע	פ	צ
YOD (I) 10	CAPH (K) 20	LAMED (L) 30	MEM (M) 40	NUN (N) 50	SAMEKH (S) 60	AYIN (O) 70	PE (P) 80	TZADDI (TZ) 90
ק	ר	ש	ת	ך	ם	ן	ף	ץ
QOPH (Q) 100	RESH (R) 200	SHIN (SH) 300	TAV (TH) 400	Final Caph 500	Final Mem 600	Final Nun 700	Final Pe 800	Final Tzaddi 900

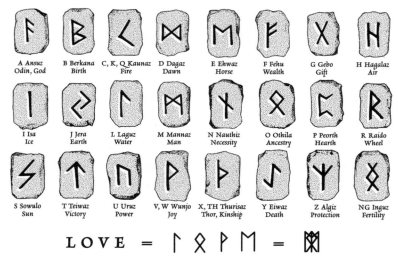

A Ansuz Odin, God	B Berkana Birth	C, K, Q Kaunaz Fire	D Dagaz Dawn	E Ehwaz Horse	F Fehu Wealth	G Gebo Gift	H Hagalaz Air
I Isa Ice	J Jera Earth	L Laguz Water	M Mannaz Man	N Nauthiz Necessity	O Othila Ancestry	P Peorth Hearth	R Raido Wheel
S Sowulo Sun	T Teiwaz Victory	U Uruz Power	V, W Wunjo Joy	X, TH Thurisaz Thor, Kinship	Y Eiwaz Death	Z Algiz Protection	NG Inguz Fertility

L O V E = ᛚ ᛟ ᚹ ᛗ = ᛗ

ABOVE: To make a Norse bind rune, a sentence or affirmation is expressed in runes. Any recuring runes are removed and then the remaining signs are placed on top or woven into each other to form a single design. Sometimes this is used as a company logo, like Bluetooth. Bind runes are found in Northern inscriptions from Iceland, Norway, and Orkney, each with their own magical implications.

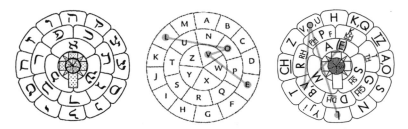

ABOVE, LEFT & RIGHT: Rosette patterns showing the Hebrew alphabet and its Latin equivalent as set out in the center of the Rose Cross lamen, worn by officers in the Hermetic Order of the Golden Dawn. By connecting certain letters, spelling out a word or the initials of a phrase, a magical shape or sigil is formed (L-O-V-E in the example shown), then used in secret. The center image shows a modern sigil wheel.

SAWS AND SAYINGS
tweets to the gods

Many of the most common spells concern money and love. However, both of these are very tricky areas to be interfering with. Spells for money don't work, as money is only an intermediary, although a spell designed to attract whatever the money was to be spent on might succeed. Trying out a love spell is never a good idea because it is acting against the will of a person to make them fall in love with someone they don't love. A better approach is for the one who wants a lover to ask that they become more loveable and attractive.

Modern spells, which dial up the required influences like a phone number, are often in verse to help remember the words. Spells must be recited from memory, not read (which is why spell books don't work). A new spell should be written and learned for each situation, working at the right phase of the moon, waxing to increase something, waning to drive harm away. The sign of the zodiac can also influence events, if used properly; but again, this is a deep study.

WHO AND HOW WILL I MARRY?

New moon, true moon,
True and bright,
If I have a true love,
Let me dream of him tonight!
If I am to marry rich,
Let me hear the cock crow!
If I am to marry poor,
Let me hear the hammer blow!

WHEN TO MARRY

Monday for wealth,
Tuesday for health,
Wednesday best day of all,
Thursday for losses,
Friday for crosses,
And Saturday no luck at all

→ SPELLS, RHYMES, AND REDES ←

TO KNOW YOUR TRUE LOVE

All hail, new moon, all hail to thee
I prithee good moon, reveal to me
This night who shall my true love be:
Who he is, and what he wears,
And what he does all months and years

TO PROTECT FROM EVIL

From Witches and Wizards,
and long-tailed Buzzards,
And creeping things
that run in hedge-bottoms,
Good Lord, deliver us!'

NEOPAGAN MORAL

Eight words the Wiccan Rede fulfill,
An it harm none do what ye will

BEARING HARD TIMES

This too shall pass

Every day, in every way, I
am getting better and better.

Chinese curse:
"May you live in interesting times!"

WISH ON A STAR

Star light, star bright,
Here's the wish I make tonight.
I wish I may, I wish I might
Achieve my wish before tonight.

LUCKY BIRTH DAYS

Monday's child is fair of face
Tuesday's child is full of grace
Wednesday's child is full of woe
Thursday's child has far to go
Friday's child is loving and giving
Saturday's child works hard for a living
But the child that is born of a Sabbath
day, is fair and wise and loves to play.

WEATHER

Red sky at night
Shepherd's delight
Red sky in the morning
Shepherd's warning

TOUCH WOOD

Knock on a tree and quietly say
To the spirit present that day
Faery fair, faery fair, wish thou me well,
Against harmful wishing weave me a spell.

SNEEZING

On Monday, sneeze for danger
On Tuesday, kiss a stranger
On Wednesday recieve a letter
On Thursday seek something better.
On Friday sneeze for sorrow
On Saturday meet your lover tomorrow
On Sunday do your safety seek
Or the devil will plague you all through the week.

SPOKEN SPELLS
the power of letters and words

Traditionally, spells are words—spoken, chanted, sung, or written with deep intent—often in an ancient or secret language. The rhythmic and repetitive sounds of words can cause shifts in consciousness which may awaken the subconscious mind and allow the spell weaver to communicate with the invisible.

Many exercises in self-awareness or confidence-boosting involve regularly speaking or singing certain phrases. Formulate your own spells by choosing a need and writing a short poem to inscribe, sing, or chant. Keep it specific and direct, be ready to pay for what you request, and give sincere thanks when your spell works. To deepen such work, use correspondences, planetary movements, and symbolism.

Some spells are statements, like *February fill the dyke, be it black or be it white!* warns of flooding, while *Rain, rain, go to Spain, and don't you dare come back again!* is a spell to bring fine weather. Some club mottoes, national anthems, or advertising slogans, like *Beanz meanz Heinz!* or *An apple a day keeps the doctor away!* can become spells if they are sung or chanted often. In this way slogans can help a team win a difficult match or encourage more people to buy a particular product.

44

→ SPOKEN SPELLS ←

CIRCLE BLESSING HAIKU
TO CLEAR A WORKING SPACE.

Power of the Earth
Form a strong foundation
To my Talisman.

Power of Water
Purify this magic circle
And keep it clear

Power of the Fire
Illuminate my working
Let it shine brightly.

Power of the Air
Bring inspiration to me
Breathe life on my charm.

Power of good Spirits
Bless this ring
and seal my spell
According to my will.

So mote it be!

HOUSE BLESSING SPELL

When you have a new home it is good
to actually sweep out with a broom the
previous occupants" influences from the
furthest room through to the front door,
which you close firmly. Then go outside
and light a candle and carry it from the
front door through every room, saying
"Let light and love fill this home."

TO EASE A BURN

Two angels came out of the West,
One brought fire, the other frost.
I ask the cooling frost to stay
but burning fire please go away.
Amen.

APPLE PEEL SPELL

Carefully peel an apple
in a single spiral
Then say:
Apple peel, apple peel, twist the rest
To show me the initial
of one who loves me best.

PINS

See a pin and pick it up
All the day will bring good luck.
See a pin and let it lie
some good luck will pass you by.

ANTI~PLAGUE SPELL

Ring a ring of roses,
A pocket full of posies,
Atishoo! Atishoo!
We all fall down.

MOON SPELL

New moon, true moon as you grow
Let my income follow through
When your face is bright and full
May my purse have plenty too.

WOVEN SPELLS
hubble bubble toil and trouble

In ancient times, sailors would seek out wise women to buy cords of wind knots. Each knot had a chant said over it, one for a gentle breeze, two for a strong wind, and three for a gale to destroy enemies. The sailor would untie the knots at sea for the desired effect and say the spell he had been taught. He would finally throw the used spell cord into the sea. Knots were also tied to symbolize unwanted blocks in a person's life, before being buried to rot away.

When writing was still seen as a magical act, spells were written and carried about, or the paper was washed and the water drunk as a way of taking in the benefit of the spell. These were made by experts, often for a specific purpose, or as sacred texts used as an amulet.

Corn dollies (*below*), woven braids, bracelets, boxes, and baskets (*opposite*), and even knitted socks and jumpers all bind the love and good wishes of the weaver into them, for fertility in the fields and protection for the wearer.

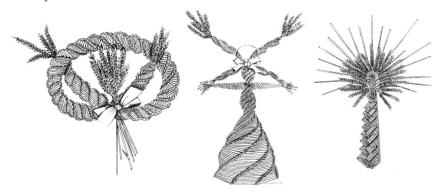

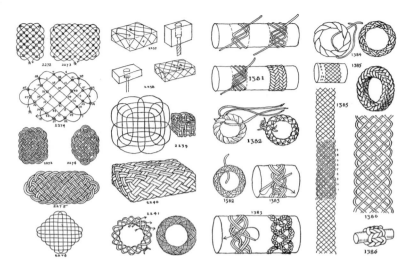

ABOVE: *Spell weaving has often involved joining, plaiting and intertwining all sorts of pliable materials whilst wishing good thoughts into the finished object. Here are a variety of woven symbols. The rings, bracelets, and floor mats are designed to unite friends and bring comfort.*

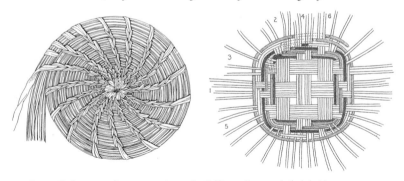

ABOVE: *Baskets woven from grasses, pine needles (left), or willow wands (right). The patterns can represent the magical spiral, expanding into a circular mat or basket base, or the weft and warp, like Yin and Yang of eternal opposites united into a magical container or simple charm of layered positive thoughts.*

MEDITATIONS
seeing with the mind's eye

Meditation is an essential skill to most esoteric practices because it gives direct access to the subconscious mind through which magic effectively works.

There are two main traditions of meditation: Eastern, where the mind is emptied and focused on to the breath to reach a state of detachment; and Western where the breath is relaxed and the mind is filled with some object of contemplation, allowing the subconscious to overflow into awareness, bringing creativity, new ideas, inspiration and illumination.

It is this key Western practice of *visualization* which is so central to effective magic. Whereas meditation is partially passive, visualization is primarily active. It requires the remembering or imagining of a scene, activity, or object with complete clarity, and then mentally encouraging an evolution to occur.

A mental journey may be followed to a new destination, a dream may be recalled to continue the story, or a real situation may be carefully considered so that a resolution may appear. It is through directed consciousness, using images, talismans, journeys to the future, or manipulating energy fields for healing, within a consecrated space, that real magic can be brought about.

The relaxation that meditation brings is also a valuable antidote to the stresses and busy activities in the modern world. It can provide a mental space and a physical silence in which true answers arise.

Learn to be careful, patient, and focused, and the unseen influences will work with you.

⇀ COMMON MEDITATION TECHNIQUES ↽

AFFIRMATION. *Verbal/visual affirmation of thing you wish to take place, e.g. confidence, health, relaxation etc.*

BALL OF LIGHT. *Visualize a golden ball of light at the center of your body to unify spirit/soul.*

BODY SCAN. *Move your awareness around your body checking and adjusting levels of energy/health/stress/relaxation.*

BREATHING. *Common practice in many Eastern traditions. Focus only on breath. Variations include counting long and short breaths, breathing only through nose/mouth/left nostril/right etc.*

CHAKRA. *Imagine body as a chain of energy flowers (or a rainbow) and work up chakras from red (base) to crown (purple).*

EMPTINESS. *Clear mind of all thoughts to approach total peace and true nature of self.*

FIVE SENSES. *Focus on five senses, sight, sound, smell, taste, and touch in turn. Then imagine these five senses as shadows of five higher senses.*

FORGETTING. *Trance state in which the ego is forgotten and awareness is only of the cosmic current. E.g. Chinese Zuowang.*

GUIDED. *Aided focus, sometimes using recorded instructions, on some thing for self-development. E.g. to boost performance, explore the subconscious, or heal a wound.*

HEART. *Focus on the heart, using visualization or synchronization of breath (including holding of breath) to heartbeats.*

KUNDALINI. *Focus on base of spine to release psychosexual serpent energy. E.g. in Tantra.*

LOVING KINDNESS. *Practice feeling kindness and good-will, toward self, family, and others.*

MANTRA. *A sound, word, or phrase which is repeated again and again until it is the only thing you are aware of. E.g. Transcendental Meditation.*

MINDFULNESS. *Observation of your perceptions and thoughts as from a third-person perspective. Often includes focus on breath.*

MOVEMENT. *Awareness of self through walking, dance & martial arts. E.g. Qigong, Yoga (conduct/postures/breathings/meditations), etc.*

OBJECT. *Full focus on a single physical object to gain understanding, contact, communication, or information. E.g. icon, photo, crystal, tree, body part, lock of hair, talisman, etc.*

PILGRIMAGE. *Normally a walking meditation, often to a sacred site. The physical journey is seen as a symbol of one's own spiritual/developmental journey.*

PRAYER. *Focus on a god, angel, or spirit with intent to converse, and offer and receive feedback of some kind, often regarding an issue.*

RETURN. *Ask what is behind something, and then what is behind that, and again, etc. Returns you to the loving center.*

SELF-INQUIRY. *Focus on "I," sometimes by continual asking of "Who am I?" Self-realization occurs as "I" is seen as the artificial dualistic construct it is.*

SOUND. *Become aware only of the sounds around you, natural etc. Includes listening to music.*

UNITY. *Focus on the unity at the center of all things.*

VISUALIZATION. *Of object, scene, scenario, or journey to help achieve a goal. E.g. a lion for strength, a waterfall for relaxation, etc.*

ZEN/ZAZEN. *Sit and practice nonthinking, by concentrating on breath, watching thoughts pass by, or using "koans."*

DREAMS
another kind of truth

Wake gently to recall your dreams so these valuable sources of inner wisdom can gradually reveal themselves to you. Some dreams are recollections of daily life, others are indications of stress (being chased), and others may be health warnings. Some people only recall black and white images, others enter a totally different world, complete with alien geology and landscapes. The Bible mentions powerful and predictive dreams later interpreted by diviners.

In a "lucid dream" you know you are dreaming and become a conscious part of the experience. Teach yourself to look at your feet when asleep; this can trigger the lucid state.

Carl Jung saw dreams as windows on the soul, with the dream objects, people, and events as *symbols*, subconscious aids to a more balanced mental state in waking life, "a spontaneous self-portrayal, in symbolic form, of the actual situation in the unconscious."

CHARACTERS FOR AN EPIC TALE

© Tom Gauld

THE SIXTH SENSE
and the art of divination

Divination covers many arts, from mental intuition to the tarot, from runes (*below left*) to scrying in a crystal ball, from interpreting omens to using inner awareness. Simply knowing that you are capable of using psychic senses can increase your chances of success. Many people discover answers or possible futures by entering a relaxed yet focused and non-judgmental state, allowing inner voices and symbols to speak to them (*see meditations, page 48*).

Dowsing (*below right*) is a very old art, originally used to locate water, but later expanded to search for minerals and pipes, and today used to find energy lines or "leys." A forked hazel or willow stick, or a pendulum may be used, with one movement for "Yes" and another for "No." Dowsing "yes" or "no" can answer questions about all sorts of things, from foods and illnesses to lost objects and deeper issues.

Information received from such sources can inspire art, music, books, foresight, the ability to heal, and general magical efficacy.

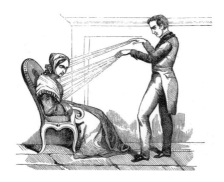

ABOVE: The symbols printed on Zener cards are used to test E.S.P. by asking subjects to guess or predict the next symbol.

LEFT: A Mesmerist using invisible influence to affect his female subject, and put her in a trance. Hypnosis, by contrast, uses spoken instructions instead of mesmeric passes.

ABOVE: The Pythia, or Oracle of Delphi, Greece, seated on her tripod over a vent in the rock from which fumes arose. These put her into a state of awareness in which she could make predictions. Potentates would send questions, which were often interpreted by priests. Prior to prophesying the Pythia would bathe in a spring, then drink from another stream and finally ice water would be poured over a goat.

MEETING THE INVISIBLE
matters of spirit

Magic relies on experience of the unseen, acknowledging the power of gods and goddesses, angels, spirits, and elementals, including tree and ancestor spirits (*below*), ghosts (*opposite top*), and fairies (*opposite bottom*), which may be encountered on occasions. Angels are messengers of God, and can be called upon for help, healing, comfort, and advice. Many old magical arts are devoted to talking to angelic beings.

Often a ritual is performed to link these realms, using incense, incantation, a magical circle of protection, and a clear purpose. Nature spirits are seen by sitting still in a wood, allowing their faces to appear in trees or among grasses. You can offer flowers, milk, honey, or wine to accompany your request. Be patient, these elementals are nervous and dance to a slower music of life.

LEFT: Ghosts may be encountered anywhere, but particularly in places steeped in history. CCTV and tourist cameras in pubs and stately homes capture them in doorways, on staircases, and above the ground, because they are between worlds. Many ghosts are in modern dress and so pass by unnoticed, or vanish when looked at directly. Some people sense presences rather than seeing figures, or notice cold areas in buildings.

BELOW: Throughout history and all over the world people have encountered faeries, elves, goblins, and otherworldly beings. Some of these are helpful, others are spiteful or destructive. Most are thought to live partly in this world and partly in another dimension which humans can occasionally enter via dreams and visions. Picture of Oberon and Titania, King and Queen of the Fairies, by Arthur Rackham.

THE MAGICAL COSMOS
everything is one

Although the arts of magic are ancient, the concepts behind their techniques are very modern. The realms we enter in dream and visionary states may be described as conscious forays into other dimensions, journeys along other time lines, or the products and experiences of other states or planes of being. Both modern scientists and ancient philosophers share the perspective that everything is connected, all parts of a great Unity, whether through gravity, an original singularity, or entangled connectivity, allowing for a small action in one place to affect everything else in the universe.

The magician Dion Fortune [1890–1946] wrote: *All gods are one god, and all goddesses are one goddess, and there is one Initiator.* Similarly, the 6th–century *Emerald Tablet* of Hermes Trismegistus states: *Those things that are above are like unto those things that are below, and those things that are below are like unto that which is above, and there is the unity of the one true thing!*

Both imply that there is a single living universe, which may contain reflections, but is never divided.

It is this connectivity which empowers the arts of magic, the skills of the diviner, the ability to heal at a distance, and many of the talents which are collected under the umbrella of parapsychology. For if everything is linked, then the connected universe easily allows for seemingly "supernatural" events to occur. And if the universe is a living entity, as the ancients believed, from the minutest atom to the entirety of the cosmos, then it may indeed also possess a Universal mind or consciousness, of which our own individual awareness is just a small part.

LEFT: An imge of the One, source of Light, pouring forth energy, here shown with the Hebrew "Yod, Heh, Vau, Heh" letters which indicate the hidden name of God. Artists have tried to delineate the ineffable, the all seeing, great Architect of the Universe. Some prefer the concept of the Great Mother or Mother Nature, but the living universe can only ever be described in purely symbolic terms.

BELOW: This familiar image shows the philosopher, alchemist, magician, or seeker striving to go beyond the limits set by logic, to reach into the heavens beyond and witness the machinery of the cosmos. Magical arts allow practitioners to interact and so alter the very structure of the perceived world. By reaching past the known limits of consciousness it is possible to communicate with the mind of the creator.

GLOSSARY OF MAGICAL TERMS

AMULET - An object, often in the shape of an eye, worn to ward off harm.

ASTRAL TRAVEL - Spiritual journeys, often during sleep, when the dreaming self leaves the physical body; sometimes called "out of the body experiences".

AURA - The energy patterns around living things, visible to witches and magicians.

BELTANE - Festival at the beginning of May, when the hawthorn (May) flowers. The name is derived from the Celtic words "Bel", good or god, and "tan", fire.

BOOK OF ILLUMINATION - A personal record of spells, poems, rituals, and other useful information collected by the magic worker.

CHAFING DISH - A flat dish on which incense is burned on charcoal.

CHAKRA - Sanskrit "wheel". One of seven energy centers running through the body.

COVEN - A group of thirteen or fewer wiccans, led by a High Priestess and High Priest. It derives from the same word as "convent".

DEOCIL - Clockwise or "godwise", this is the direction the Sun appears to move in the sky.

DISCARNATE - Not alive on Earth, as ghosts or angels.

DIVINATION - The many arts of consulting the "divinity", reading Tarot cards, seeking water, or consulting oracles.

DOWSING - From the old Cornish, "to seek", especially water or buried treasure, using a Y-shaped hazel dowsing wand.

EPHEMERIS - This is a list of tables of positions of the planets, the Sun and Moon, used by astrologers.

EQUINOX - The time of year when day and night are equal.

GOLDEN MEAN - This is a ratio which occurs widely in nature, in the patterns of leaves and in the proportions of the human body. It can be approximated as 5:8.

HERMETIC MYSTERIES - Hermes was the Greek God of Wisdom, based on the Egyptian God, Thoth, who gave the understanding of magic to humankind. Mysteries are things which cannot be told, only experienced.

HOLY or **HOLEY STONES** - These are stones, sometimes fossil sponges, which have natural holes right through them. For hundreds of years they have been hung by red wool or ribbon to bring luck.

IMBOLC - A festival in early February when ewes lamb. Imbolc means "in the belly" in the Celtic tongue. The festival is also called Candlemas or the Feast of St Bride.

INNER PLANE ADEPT - Otherworldly teacher: some are discarnate wise people; others are angels.

KARMA - Sanskrit word for fate or balance. Every action accrues spiritual prom or loss, and through a series of reincarnated lives the balance must be worked out.

KEY OF SOLOMON - A book from the Middle Ages which sets out how talismans are to be made and which symbols should be used, and gives the basis of some rituals.

LODGE - A group of magicians meet in a lodge, as do Freemasons. It is a term used for both the buildingor temple and the group itself.

PENTACLE - A five-sided shape ("penta" is Greek for five); as opposed to a pentagram, which has five points.

PSYCHOMETRIZE To sense by touch the history of an object or information about its owner.

QABALAH - One of the three spellings for an ancient Hebrew system of philosophy, wisdom, and magic. These are the Jewish Kabbalah, the Christian Cabala and the mystical Qabalah. The variations come from transliterating the Hebrew letters QBL into English.

QUERENT - In a divination situation, the querent is the one asking a question that the diviner is trying to answer.

SCRY - Derived from the French "descrier", to proclaim, scrying means divining by crystal-gazing. A scrying glass is a crystal ball.

SHAMAN - Originally one from a tribe in Siberia in Russia, who worked with magic and spirits. Having experienced death, a shaman can recall the souls of the sick.

SIDEREAL TIME - Star time. Used by many astrologers as the time frame from which they calculate the positions of the planets and stars in a horoscope. It differs slightly from "clock" time.

SOLSTICE - At midsummer and midwinter the Sun reaches its highest and lowest points of its cycle, giving each hemisphere of the world its shortening and lengthening days.

SPECULUM - A speculum is any kind of gazing glass or scrying ball, such as a crystal ball or black mirror, used to see into the future or from a distance.

SUNWISE - Clockwise. To open a ritual space, it is usual to walk circles clockwise, sunwise, or deocil. Close the circle or space by walking anticlockwise.

TALISMAN - A deliberately-made object which draws on the power and symbols of the planets or signs of the zodiac, often using archaic writing, to bring about a single specific purpose.

THURIBLE - An incense burner, often on chains so it can be swung to cense a ritual space. These are often carried in processions.

TREE OF LIFE - A diagram consisting of 10 spheres connected by 22 paths showing the spiritual evolution of creation. It is central to the Qabalah, and is used by many western magicians as a kind of road map, showing where planetary or angelic powers may be located.

WLDDERSHINS - Anticlockwise, from a Scottish dialect word. The Earth actually turns this way, making the Sun appear to move clockwise. Circles are walked widdershins to close down the power at the end of a ritual.

ZENER CARDS - Special cards with clear shapes of a circle, square, cross, star, as well as wavy lines, used to test extra sensory perception or psychic power.